# BUSINESSWOMAN

## Your Guide to Entrepreneurial Success

# DANI WHITESTONE

Copyright © 2021 by Dani Whitestone

All rights reserved. No part of this publication may be reproduced, distributed, or transmitted in any form or by any means, including photocopying, recording, or other electronic or mechanical methods, without the prior written permission of the publisher, except in the case of brief quotations embodied in reviews and certain other noncommercial uses permitted by copyright law.

Cover and interior design: Dino Marino, www.dinomarino.com

ISBN Print: 978-1-7366323-0-7

ISBN eBook: 978-1-7366323-1-4

# THE BRILLIANT BUSINESSWOMAN

Your Guide to Entrepreneurial Success

Dani Whitestone

## SPECIAL INVITATION & BONUS FOR YOU

It can be lonely being an entrepreneur and there's always so much to learn! This is your personal invitation to join my online community and thriving network of like-minded women entrepreneurs. You'll love how we all support each other and grow together. With monthly networking opportunities and featured guest experts, there's always something fun going on! You can find The Women's Small Business & Leadership Network at www.daniwhitestone.com/connect.

As a bonus and thank you for reading this book, I've created a handy business startup checklist to help set you up for success when building your business. To get your free download, visit www.daniwhitestone.com/startupchecklist.

## DEDICATION

This book is dedicated to my Mom & Dad

Mom, thank you for being a stubborn,
independent weirdo who doesn't worry
about what people think of you.

Dad, thank you for believing I could do anything,
even when people told you I couldn't
because I was a girl.

Love you.

# Table of Contents

**INTRODUCTION** ............................................. I

**1. YOU'VE GOT THIS!** ..................................... 1
- You Can Be a Successful Entrepreneur .......... 3
- It's a Leap of Faith ............................................ 4
- Watch Out for Fear Dumping ........................ 5

**2. SET YOURSELF UP FOR SUCCESS** ........... 6
- Carefully Cultivate Your Environment .......... 8
- Assemble Your Dream Team ........................... 9
- An Attitude of Gratitude ............................... 10
- You Are Enough ............................................ 11

**3. DARE TO DREAM** ....................................... 13
- Get It Down on Paper ................................... 15
- What Problem Does Your Business Solve? ... 16
- What if My Business Idea Already Exists? ... 17
- Test the Waters .............................................. 19
- Beware of Shiny Objects ................................ 20
- Thank the Inner Voice .................................. 21

## 4. GET READY TO LAUNCH ............... 22
Find Your Niche ............................................ 23
How to Name Your Business ..................... 24
Brand Identity Basics .................................. 27
Protect Yourself ............................................ 29
Have Good Contracts and Agreements ....... 30
Find out What Insurance You Need ............ 30
Trademarks ................................................... 31
Save Time with Systems ............................... 32

## 5. PREPARE FOR PROFITS ............... 33
Money is a Tool ............................................ 34
Plan Your Pricing ......................................... 36
Get Unstuck .................................................. 37
The Discount Dilemma ............................... 38

## 6. CREATE CONNECTIONS: MARKETING & SALES ............... 40
It's All About the Customer ....................... 41
So . . . What Do You Do? ........................... 43
Progress, Not Perfection ............................. 44
What's a Sales Funnel? ................................ 45
Communicate with Care ............................. 48

## 7. GET READY TO GROW ............ 50

Bank on the Basics ..................... 53

Fantastically Free ....................... 55

Low-Cost Leverage ..................... 59

Make Money Marketing .............. 62

Free Samples, Trials,
and Money-Back Guarantees ...... 64

Measure Your Marketing ............ 65

## 8. TAKING CARE OF YOUR MOST PRECIOUS BUSINESS ASSET-YOU! ........ 67

A Healthy Business Starts
with a Healthy Owner ................. 68

The Entrepreneurial Athlete ........ 69

Listen When Your Body Talks..... 70

Your Invisible Army ................... 72

Freeing Yourself from Guilt ........ 74

## 9. INVESTING IN YOURSELF ........ 75

You Are Worth It ....................... 77

How to Find the Right Coach ..... 77

Keep Moving Forward ................ 79

## FINAL THOUGHTS AND RESOURCES....... 80
### Books to Inspire and Educate ..................... 82
### Websites and Resources .............................. 82

## CONNECT WITH ME ................................... 83

## ACKNOWLEDGMENTS ............................... 84

## ABOUT DANI ............................................... 85

## AUTHOR'S NOTES........................................ 86

## CONTINUE YOUR JOURNEY ...................... 87

# Introduction

*"Don't sit down and wait for the opportunities to come. Get up and make them."*

Madame C. J. Walker

If you are picking up this book, it means you are thinking about—or are already on—the crazy ride that is entrepreneurship. Congratulations are in order because it is no small feat! Launching and growing a small business can be one of the most exhilarating things you'll ever do. But it can also drive you nuts and have you second-guessing everything.

As a serial entrepreneur, I have a passion for helping women successfully create, launch, and grow their small businesses. My goal in writing this book is to instill in you the belief that you truly can do this and give you some hard-earned knowledge and tools to succeed.

It's frustrating to see brilliant women with so much to offer make common business and marketing mistakes that prevent them from reaching their goals. Reading this book will save you a lot of time, money, and stress—getting you from where you are to where you want to be faster.

Will you still encounter some pitfalls? Absolutely. I don't know of a single successful businesswoman who hasn't had their butt kicked on their way to success. However, I hope that by reading this book, you'll be better equipped to handle the challenges ahead.

As an entrepreneur, you get to live your true purpose and make the world a better place by sharing your unique gifts every day. There's nothing better. So, dream as big as you dare and watch your amazing life unfold!

# 1

## You've Got This!

*"If the path before you is clear,
you're probably on someone else's."*

Joseph Campbell

On the way to where I am now, I've certainly had a lot of twists, turns, and unexpected adventures. The path wasn't very clear. I had the goal of being a successful business owner and self-made millionaire by the age of thirty-five—and achieved that—but at times, I had no clue how it was all going to come together. It's hard to have dreams of grandeur when you're working as the Easter Bunny at the mall and sleeping on your best friend's floor!

Going after your goals, despite people telling you what they think you should do, is the key. When you do this, the universe conspires to help you in the weirdest ways.

For example, when I was little, I wanted to play the trumpet, but I wasn't allowed to because I was "a girl." So, when my younger brother was allowed to play, I stole it from him every chance I could and practiced like crazy. By the time I was in ninth grade, I was a good enough trumpet player to get hired for the musical *Oklahoma* for a local theater production. When I arrived, I sat down next to a fellow freshmen clarinet player with similar entrepreneurial aspirations who would become my future business partner. Together we built and sold an incredibly successful legal software company, which allowed me to achieve my goal!

I have countless stories like this, and they've all led to the amazingly fulfilling life that I enjoy today. Do I listen to well-intentioned advice and seek out guidance? Certainly, but I always consider the source and forge ahead for what I think the right thing is *for me*.

## YOU CAN BE A SUCCESSFUL ENTREPRENEUR

Successful entrepreneurs come in all shapes and sizes. We're tall, short, old, young, broke (when we start), rich, married, single, and are every color under the rainbow. So, whoever you are, you can become a successful entrepreneur!

While we all look different, we do have similar character traits that help us reach our versions of success. These include passion, resilience, empathy, flexibility, and doing tasks we don't feel like doing. Being self-motivated, creative, and a good communicator also certainly helps.

But just as there are positive traits that will help, there are traits that won't serve you in your entrepreneurial goals—things like being a control freak and never delegating, not having clear boundaries, or working yourself to exhaustion. To be sure, we are all far from perfect, but knowing where we tend to struggle and need help is a great first step to doing better and reaching our goals.

## IT'S A LEAP OF FAITH

One of my favorite movie scenes that sums up what entrepreneurship is like is in *Indiana Jones and the Last Crusade*. (Go ahead and search for "Indiana Jones Leap of Faith" to see what I'm talking about.) You'll see our hero in all his dramatic glory come to the edge of a huge chasm, which he must cross to save his father. Our reluctant hero realizes that to get across, the task at hand is to literally take "a leap of faith." It just looks like he's going to step out and fall to certain death. We watch as he battles his fears and doubts until he centers himself into a state of calm. He then extends one foot and steps off the cliff . . . and onto the invisible bridge that was there all along.

That's what entrepreneurship is like. Taking that next step toward your goals and trusting you have a bridge to carry you across even though you will sometimes be full of fear and doubt.

## WATCH OUT FOR FEAR DUMPING

Imagine you're at a cookout on a beautiful, sunny day, and you start telling your family about your business idea. You are full of energy and excitement as you lay out your fantastic vision.

Then it happens. They start telling you about Aunt Patty and how she started a business a million years ago, and when it failed, her whole life fell apart, and she spent the last of her lonely days wandering the town half-naked and living off cat food.

Perhaps you've already experienced the phenomenon—the joy of being shot down when you've shared your ideas with others. It can be confusing and heartbreaking when it comes from people close to you—people such as your partner, friends, or family. While they are likely sharing their stories and concerns with good intentions, it doesn't make it any more pleasant to have the wind taken from your newly hoisted sail. Even if you encounter resistance, as hard as it might be, stay true to your dreams and goals. Don't take it to heart when others dump their fears all over you. Make sure you have a support network of like-minded entrepreneurs to help keep the wind in that sail.

# 2

## Set Yourself Up for Success

*"The road to success is always under construction."*

Lily Tomlin

Here's a million-dollar question. Do you love your hobby, or do you love business? Can you love both? Absolutely! But let's clarify this a bit. Let's say you love knitting scarves. Not only do you love your scarf creations, but everyone around you loves them too. You get constant requests for your scarves, and come Christmastime, you feel like your arms are going to fall off from all the knitting, but you still love it.

Then one day, someone tells you that you should do this as a full-time business. You think to yourself, *My god, that would be amazing! I'd get to knit to my heart's content and be my own boss!* So, you decide to give it a go.

You suddenly get the very rude wake-up call that if you turn your hobby into a business, there's a lot less time to do what you love, as "the business" creeps in. You need to make decisions like how to price your scarves and where and how to sell them. The next thing you know, you've spent $600 on a website that doesn't work—and your tech guy, Fred, left the country for a month to be with his new online girlfriend. You are trying to deal with all of this while fulfilling the large order you just landed for your local store.

I am a *huge* champion for anyone launching their own small business, but I am an even *more huge* advocate of not sugar coating anything (except for donuts). I wish I could tell you that everyone would love running their own business, but this isn't the case. To be successful in business, you need to not only enjoy your hobby but also enjoy business and rising to the unique challenges it presents.

If, after some research and soul-searching, you find that keeping your full-time job and pursuing your passion as a side hustle is the way to go for right now or even forever, that is still a great option. You are still awesome, and you'll still be a business owner!

## CAREFULLY CULTIVATE YOUR ENVIRONMENT

You can think of your life and business as a precious garden. For it to thrive, you need to be constantly removing weeds that will steal nutrients and stunt the fruit you are trying to grow. Jim Rohn says, "You are the average of the five people you spend the most time with." I believe this is true.

Every year, I go on a solo retreat to clear my head. I reflect on which people around me are positive and fill me with energy to reach my goals, and which of them drain me and weigh me down. In other words, who provides nutrients for my garden? And who are the weeds?

It can be difficult to let people go, especially when they've played important roles in your life. But if you truly want to reach your goals, these are the tough decisions that you need to make. This does not mean that some are bad people who need to be completely removed from your life, but you might need to do some pruning for your garden to flourish. It's my personal experience that when I do this, the most amazing new people show up at just the right time to help me create the amazing life I am heading towards.

## ASSEMBLE YOUR DREAM TEAM

John Maxwell says, "The bigger the dream, the bigger the team." So, who are your go-to people who will support you in your new adventure? Those are the people who will help carry you through your challenges and celebrate your victories. We all know some friends who are not the right go-to people for this. I want you to have a list of people you can depend on for hugs and well-deserved celebrations.

When it comes to hiring professionals, invest in the best you can find and afford. Having something done right the first time is always less expensive than doing it twice. Some professionals to be on the lookout for include an accountant, bank agent, bookkeeper, business attorney, business coach or mentor, graphic designer, human resources or employment consultant, insurance agent, and a webmaster or someone who can provide tech support.

## AN ATTITUDE OF GRATITUDE

One practice to which I credit my general cheery demeanor and overall sanity is having an attitude of gratitude. When you come to appreciate things like having a warm bed to sleep in and access to clean water, it's harder to get upset at life's little annoyances. When I reflect on how fortunate I am to live the life I do, it always fills my heart.

It's not just being grateful for the big things, but really taking time to savor everyday little things as well. Whether it's appreciating the warmth of the sun through a window or the feeling of grass between your toes, savoring those moments can help you find balance and counteract the hectic pace you can get caught up in as an entrepreneur.

Though harder to do, I've also come to be grateful for all my hardships and heartaches as they've all held valuable lessons. Many of these lessons were the foundation for my future successes. If you are going through a tough time, it helps to find meaning in the struggle. While it may be hard to be grateful in the moment, you may be able to look back with gratitude at the person you've become because of your challenges.

## YOU ARE ENOUGH

Close your eyes and imagine, just for one fleeting moment, that you are enough just as you are. What if you were at complete peace with yourself? No matter your perceived flaws and imperfections, you are perfectly awesome.

I've learned there's power in self-acceptance, and I believe everyone is walking around doing the best they can with what they have; you and I are no exception. It doesn't mean that you can't have goals and desires to change in some way, but realize that you are beautiful and amazing wherever you are starting. Realize how awesome you are at just being you.

If you have regrets and wish you could have handled a situation better, there's no sense in beating yourself up. Endlessly berating yourself won't bring you closer to your goals. It's much better to reflect on lessons learned with love in your heart for yourself and know that you'll do that much better next time.

Remember as you go forward, building your business, that your worth as a person is independent of any of your accomplishments, business or otherwise. You are enough, and you are loved just as you are.

# 3

## Dare to Dream

*"A ship is safe in harbor,
but that's not what ships are for."*

John A. Shedd

If you can dream it, you can make it happen. However, it will help if you make your vision as clear as you can. If you do that, you'll see opportunities that will help you reach your goals and be less prone to distraction.

Start by creating a vision board, digital or physical, so you can actually see what you want to achieve. It's also a great source of inspiration to turn to when the going gets tough, when you need to remember *why* you are doing this. So, start thinking about what you want your life to be. Get that inspiration out of your head and onto your vision board.

I've always done this with amazing results I achieved my dream of becoming a self-made millionaire and did it completely in service to others through my business. It's insanely rewarding. And really, there's nothing particularly special about me. My parents weren't entrepreneurs. I waitressed my way through college, and I self-funded all my businesses. Most people around me (family included) told me I was crazy, and I should "just go get a normal job." But I built and sold a successful legal software company anyway. So, trust me, you've got this!

## GET IT DOWN ON PAPER

We are more likely to achieve our goals if they are written down—so take some time with your computer or a good old-fashioned notebook and start getting clear on what you want to accomplish. Some questions you can ask yourself are:

- What's my dream life?
- When I look back on my life when I'm 103, what do I want to have accomplished?
- How much money do I want to make per year?
- What are my love and relationship goals?
- What are my spiritual and health goals?
- What are my "this would just be totally awesome to do" goals?
- What impact do I want to have on my community and the world?

You need to give this some serious thought, so you don't accidentally build something you hate. And yep, I did this too. One of my first official businesses was a music booking agency. Soon after launch, I found myself working days, nights, and weekends—being screamed at by overly stressed mothers-of-the-bride and giving directions to hopelessly lost bagpipe players. If I had given serious thought to what I wanted my life to be like, I would not have created that business.

This is your life, and you get to map it out through your business. If you love to travel, set your business up so you can. The same goes if you don't want to work on Fridays. Your business needs to support you and the life you want to live. That's one of the most rewarding and exciting parts of being an entrepreneur.

## WHAT PROBLEM DOES YOUR BUSINESS SOLVE?

For your business to succeed, it needs to help solve a problem or fill a need. Whether that is making us look awesome under a dress (Spanx), helping women launch and grow businesses (me), or making your house smell like an apple pie, even though you haven't baked one in five years (Yankee Candle), you need to figure out why someone would need or want to buy what you have.

If you are fortunate enough to have a few early customers or super fans, ask them why they bought from you. What problem did your product or service solve? How did it make them feel? What transformation did they experience because of working with you? At the deepest level, our products or services need to help people survive and thrive.

For your marketing to be effective, you need to go deeper into those problems you solve. We're all inclined and comfortable to talk about surface problems, but you'll stand out if you are talking about the real issues people are having. For example, my last company developed and sold legal document automation software, but I didn't sell "software." I sold attorneys the ability to get home in time to read their kids a bedtime story. My software didn't just allow them to process their paperwork faster (surface problem); it allowed them to have precious time with their children and prevented them from living with parental guilt and shame. Now *that's* solving a problem.

## WHAT IF MY BUSINESS IDEA ALREADY EXISTS?

Now let's pretend that you've got your idea and you are super excited to get going. But you soon encounter someone doing that exact same thing you planned to do. Before you go into a downward spiral of misery, thinking your world is coming to an end, stop! Because this is great news.

Hear me out. It's awesome because someone else has already proven your concept works. You have the opportunity to move forward knowing there is a need for your product or service, and you can even create a more profitable niche for yourself.

For example, what if you are a massage therapist and you move to a town that already has twenty other therapists? You could just hang up your oils and get another job, but what if it really means you picked a high-demand area with a widespread knowledge of the benefits of massage and the money to pay for it? That's a huge perspective shift.

As a massage therapist, what if your favorite people to work with are babies? You might position yourself as a specialist in neonatal massage. Now, if you are a mom with an infant looking for a massage, are you going to go to "Kevin's Massage" or "Julie's Neonatal Massage"?

Unless the new mom has a great existing relationship with Kevin, she is going to call you. And when she comes in the door, you wow her and give her free twenty-minute massage trial certificates to give to all her mom friends, which she happily does at her next "Baby and Me" class.

And guess what? You *are* a specialist, so while others might charge $80 for a massage, you get to charge $120, and the moms gladly pay it, knowing that their precious babies are in expert hands. (The specialty organic baby lotions you sell at checkout don't hurt your bottom line either!)

## TEST THE WATERS

I once met with a wonderful woman looking to go out on her own in business for the first time. She made beautiful, handcrafted glass jewelry. She'd been looking at retail space and was so excited at the prospect of having a store of her own. According to the numbers, if she sunk her life savings into it, she'd be able to afford the lease for a year. That was *before* all the other costs associated with retail space.

I spoke with her about taking a lower-risk approach to exploring the market for her jewelry while building up an audience and some experience for her full-time venture. She listened as we explored her options, such as starting out at some craft fairs to see what kind of people were drawn to her jewelry. Were they funky millennials or men wanting something unique for the special women in their lives? What colors sold the best? What pieces seemed to sit and never sell?

Gaining market data, whether in person, at a fair, or online, is invaluable before committing to huge overhead expenses. It hurts my heart when I see little shops open and close within months, knowing that those owners are likely still on the hook for a lease for tens of thousands of dollars. Don't let this be you!

## BEWARE OF SHINY OBJECTS

Clarifying your business focus is crucially important. It will keep you from "shiny object syndrome." That's the tendency for entrepreneurs to get excited about the next big thing, take on too much, and stretch themselves and their resources way too thin. I, too, fall victim to this because *I get so excited* about doing, learning, and offering new things! But when I take on too much, everything, including my health, suffers.

Don't get me wrong. As business owners, we certainly need to keep aware of opportunities and make adjustments for our business to thrive. But pursuing too many new ventures at once, or ones that are not our core focus and competency, can spell disaster. These decisions need to be made very carefully and strategically.

## THANK THE INNER VOICE

We all have an inner voice that freaks the heck out when we do something new. The wonderful book, *The Confidence Gap: A Guide to Overcoming Fear and Self-Doubt* by Russ Harris, embraces the fact that we all have this voice in our heads, and it doesn't mean anything is wrong with us.

He explains that our brains are constantly scanning the environment for danger and always trying to protect us. Russ's advice is to thank the brain for its work in trying to keep us alive, but also acknowledge that even if it feels like we are about to be mauled by a tiger when doing something new, like starting a business, it is unlikely that we will actually die.

Because we all have this issue to varying degrees, including successful entrepreneurs, don't let self-doubt or imposter syndrome get in the way of going for your dreams. What I can tell you is that having experience certainly makes things easier, but you only get there by showing up and being very uncomfortable at times. However, if that inner voice is still holding you back, invest in tools and therapies to help. Don't let this be the thing that keeps you from making your dreams a reality. You and your dreams are just too precious!

# 4

# Get Ready to Launch

*"Life is either a daring adventure or nothing at all."*

Hellen Keller

Not knowing where to start when launching a business is completely normal. Let's walk through some business fundamentals to put your mind at ease and reassure yourself that you are well on your way to becoming a successful business owner.

## FIND YOUR NICHE

Once you have an idea of what your business will be and what problem it will solve, defining who you will serve is the most powerful thing you can do to help your company grow and for your marketing to work. Unfortunately, it is also the number one thing that drives my clients bonkers.

Picking a niche can be tricky for a small business owner because it feels counterintuitive. It's hard to narrow down and commit to one small segment of a market since it can seem like you are leaving out potential buyers. But if you are trying to sell and speak to everyone, your message will be so general, diluted, and weak you won't get anyone's attention, and in reality, you'll end up speaking to no one.

Take me, for example. I could have marketed myself as a "coach," but my passion and expertise are in business, so I'm a "business coach." Since this is still yawn-worthy, I decided to focus on women, which makes me a "Women's Business Coach." And since my skillset and passion is for small business, I'm a "Women's Small Business Coach." Focusing on this niche is how you've come to read this book today.

Doing the hard work and picking a niche has many benefits. Most importantly, it allows you to speak your customers' language. The words you use to market your business will be very different if your target market is tween girls versus 50-year-old men. By using the language of your target market, you cut through the noise, and your ideal customer will read your words and think, *Ah! This is for me!*

Another benefit of picking a niche is you'll know where to reach your ideal clients. What social media platforms do they use? Do they frequent salons or plumbing supply stores? Once you know who you are serving, you can find the right places to reach them. It's a crucial piece of information to get the most out of your marketing dollar.

## HOW TO NAME YOUR BUSINESS

Putting careful thought into naming your business is a smart way to position yourself for future success. If you have a name in mind, see if anyone else is already using it. Good places to start are with your town or city clerk's office and the office of your secretary of state.

Your next consideration should be finding a business name that is easy to remember, easy to pronounce, and preferably, easy to spell. You don't want a prospective client's first impression of you to be one of confusion. Not to mention, if they can't easily say or type your name, they will be less likely to refer others to you. You may also want to consider if a website domain for your prospective business is available.

Naming your business something clear tells people what you do without spending a dime. For example, if you have a new puppy tearing apart your house, which business would you call: "Cathy and Coco's Dream" (named for Cathy's first dog, Coco, and her dream of having a dog training business someday), or "Cathy's Reliable Dog Training"? The latter isn't sexy, but it's clear. Without a million-dollar budget to build up your brand like *Nike*, choosing an effective name is a great move for many small businesses. One consideration before choosing a descriptive name is that it will be harder to trademark, so be sure to consult a trademark attorney for more information if this is important to you.

*What you want in a name:*

- Legally available
- Easy to read and understand
- Website domain available
- Something that clarifies what your business does (but note the potential trademark challenge)
- Something that sounds good when spoken out loud
- A name that you are personally happy with

*What I have seen and oh so tactfully tried to talk people out of:*

- Names that are hard to spell
- Names that are hard to pronounce
- A name that only makes sense to you
- Anything you have to spend time explaining to people

## BRAND IDENTITY BASICS

When you are just starting out, it can be easy to say, "I'll figure out my branding later," but putting some care and thought into your brand identity now will make your marketing much more effective. Branding is a *huge* topic, and we will only scratch the surface here, talking specifically about brand identity, but this should help get you started.

Your brand identity is way more than just your logo. It emotionally conveys who you are and what you're about, allowing you to stand out in your market. The power of a great brand identity is that it immediately sets expectations for what your prospective customer will experience when working with you, even before reading any of your marketing material. If your brand identity is cohesive, it creates trust, which leads to sales. If your brand is a bit of a mishmash of stuff that doesn't make any sense, that also sets a tone (and likely one you don't want.)

The parts of your brand identity that should play well together are your logo, brand graphics, colors, fonts, and images. Each part deserves careful consideration because it's going to speak to your customers *way* before you get a chance to.

Do you want to convey that you are super modern or classic, luxury or affordable, silly or serious?

Even though we usually want to bring our personality into our brand as small business owners, we must ensure our brand will resonate with our prospective customers. Since the clients of my legal software company were all attorneys, our brand identity was polished, professional, used classic fonts and a lot of blue tones. But when I started my coaching company for women entrepreneurs, I busted out the pink and funky scripts.

Once you have your logo and branding together, use it everywhere! It will help your emerging business start to be recognized, and that consistency will help you build trust. Even in your social media images, stick your logo in one of the corners, so your brand gets seen as people scroll and swipe on by.

You can hire professionals to help pull this together for you because there is a lot involved. But if that is not in your budget, do the best with what you have based on your skills and research. Your company will still be in a stronger position for having invested the time.

## PROTECT YOURSELF

One way to protect yourself and your assets is to incorporate your business. There are many ways to do this, so consult your attorney and accountant to make sure you get the correct business structure for you. Though these entities will protect you and your assets similarly, they will treat your income differently. Ideally, your attorney and accountant will speak to each other to ensure they do the right thing for your circumstances.

You may have heard of something called a DBA, which stands for "Doing Business As" or FBN, "Fictitious Business Name." If you are operating under another name different from your own, you may be required to register one of these in your city or town. Registering a DBA or FBN is normally simple to do and inexpensive. The downside is that it offers you no legal protection.

To ensure you are protected, not only does your business need to be incorporated correctly, but it also needs to be properly maintained each year for it to keep its power. If you mess up and forget to maintain it during the year, you open yourself up to something called "piercing the corporate veil," meaning whoever is suing you can blast past the wall that used to be your corporation and come after your house. So,

I highly recommend finding a good business attorney who is used to working with small business owners.

## HAVE GOOD CONTRACTS AND AGREEMENTS

You'll need various contracts and agreements to run your business, and they will undoubtedly get better as your business grows and develops. You'll need to do some research into which contracts are standard in your industry. It is inevitable when doing business that disputes will arise, and clearly written contracts and agreements will serve you well. Good contracts benefit both parties because they bring clarity to your business transaction, so don't be bashful about requiring them.

## FIND OUT WHAT INSURANCE YOU NEED

Having some manner of business insurance (even if it is not mandatory) is smart. What you need will vary depending upon where you are and what you do. This will take a little research on your part, and for many low-risk professionals, insurance is not that expensive.

For example, if you are a health coach, you'll need some manner of professional liability insurance in case you recommend someone eats bananas, and they have an allergic reaction and sue you. Also, if you have physical space, and the next guy walks into your office and slips on the aforementioned banana peel and breaks his leg, that's where general liability insurance would apply.

## TRADEMARKS

Getting a trademark can be a smart move to protect your brand identity. However, the ins and outs of it can be quite complicated and time-consuming. If you have concerns, get referred to a trusted trademark attorney and see if they offer a free consultation. What you don't want to have happen is for you to set up your glorious brand and website only to get a scary cease and desist letter.

My personal experience with this is that it was too complicated and costly to pursue the trademark for the original name of our legal software, so we switched names and went with the trademark for "TurboLaw" instead. After some negotiation and a written agreement with a much larger company with a similar name (and a lot of praying), to our delight, we were finally granted this trademark on my birthday. The universe can be funny like that.

## SAVE TIME WITH SYSTEMS

As you are starting out, you'll be wearing many hats. Having systems in place can save you a lot of time and prevent mistakes. I highly recommend documenting your routine tasks and creating checklists from the very beginning, keeping them updated as they evolve. Doing this will not only free up mental bandwidth, but it will also be all set up for you to hand off to someone else.

# 5

## Prepare for Profits

*"I feel like money makes you more of who you already are."*

Sara Blakely

If you want to make money, *you have to be okay with making money.* Seems easy enough, right? But since I grew up in a household where it wasn't "polite to talk about money," my comfort level around it was understandably lacking. Many of us have hidden mental money messages that are holding us back and sabotaging our success. It's a good idea to explore your beliefs about money to ensure that they do not block your financial success.

## MONEY IS A TOOL

I once had a friend who told me she desperately wanted to earn more money but didn't want to be a bad person. Each month brought her financial stress, and it was difficult to make ends meet. She believed that as long as she struggled financially, she remained a "good person."

The truth is, no matter how much she earned, no amount of money would have ever made her a bad person. She'd still be a great person who lived life with a lot less stress and would use those financial resources to do more good.

Let's play fill in the blank to see how many of these common sayings and beliefs are embedded into your brain.

- Money is the root of all _____.
- Money doesn't grow on _____.
- A day late and a dollar _____.
- A penny saved is a penny _____.

Answers: Evil. Trees. Short. Earned.

How did you do? If you've ever heard or thought any of these things, you're not alone. Even if you don't believe them all, they're still stuck in your head.

How would your life be different if you made the money you wanted? Would you be less stressed and healthier? Who else could you help if you made more money? Money is just a tool. Just as water can do great things like bring life to gardens, it can also be used for harm. Money is the same way; it all depends on how it's used. If you are a good person, having as much money as you want will bring more goodness into the world.

Another important part of your business and financial success is determining how much money you want to earn. Saying "I want to be rich" won't cut it. You need a definite number so you know how to structure your business to hit your goal. It doesn't matter if it's $30,000 or $3 million a year. You need a goal to make it your reality.

So, how much would you like to make in a year? If you have hang-ups about money, just jot down a number that excites you before your brain chimes in. That will be a great starting point!

## PLAN YOUR PRICING

In any type of business, you'll find people who make a ton of money and people who are broke. Some yoga teachers are millionaires, while others struggle to make ends meet. I've also seen women work just as hard to earn $15,000 a year as those who earn $500,000, so why not set up your business model to reach your financial goals?

If you aren't comfortable with numbers and calculations, this is a great opportunity to have coffee with someone who is—and have some fun. Your mission is to find a pricing model for your goods and services to support your income goal.

The trick is to work with "net" profits here. (That means the money you get to keep after expenses). The last thing you want to realize after months of being in business is that you are losing money on each sale!

As you play with the numbers, realize that the scenario can go one of two ways. Some women are happy because they realize their dream goal is totally doable, while others are sad because the math doesn't work. Congrats either way! Seeing the numbers as an achievable goal is a huge motivator. And seeing that the math doesn't work to reach your goals is way better than finding it out in a year. Adjust your business plan *now* to make the numbers work.

## GET UNSTUCK

I once had an amazing client who was stuck launching her coaching business because she was afraid to charge what people were telling her she "should" be charging for her services. Because this number intimidated her, it had her frozen in her tracks. I knew if we did not find a solution, she'd delay her launch for months.

I asked her, "What do you feel comfortable charging right now in order to launch?"

She gave it some thought for a moment and answered, "$99 per hour." While we were on the phone together, she launched her business and, within two weeks, had five clients and was *ready to raise her pricing.* Forward action got her "unstuck," and the money started rolling in. We just needed to get her going!

## THE DISCOUNT DILEMMA

Using discounts can either help or harm your business. Strategic promotions can earn you more business. But using discounts indiscriminately will devalue your products and services, so no one takes you seriously. I love when small business owners use discounts and promotions as part of a well-thought-out marketing strategy and not as an act of desperation. Having a discounted introductory offer can be an effective, low-risk way for people to try your products and services. Including a promotional item with the purchase, such as a free gift, book, or bonus session, can also be a great way to add value and encourage a sale.

When I took over the marketing for my legal software company, I stopped the discounts immediately. Before that, there was a bargain-basement cheesy "sale" every week, which would never gain us respect or trust within our target market of legal professionals. However, we used free trials of our software to huge success.

Here's another cautionary tale about discounting that I witnessed first-hand. I once took myself on a spa weekend at a historic luxury hotel using a fantastically low promotional deal. I enjoyed a eucalyptus steam room and was in mineral bath heaven. As I left my bliss and headed to my room, I passed by a woman at the spa's front desk screaming at the staff. She had stormed in without an appointment demanding immediate service, putting her bare feet up on the counter to show them how badly she needed a pedicure. It would appear she was not the target customer the spa was used to serving, and the scene was certainly out of place for that establishment.

What do you think the cost to that business was for running the discount? The customer was unhappy, the staff was unhappy, and the awful scene gave a horrible impression to other guests. Of course, the hotel was already earning less per room because of the discount.

Long story short, the hotel ended up attracting customers not in their target market because of that promotion, and they no doubt realized it because I never saw that offer again!

# 6

# Create Connections: Marketing & Sales

*"I've learned that people will forget what you said,
people will forget what you did,
but people will never forget how you made them feel."*

Maya Angelou

When someone asks me to "teach them marketing," it's a bit like being asked to describe the ocean. Do you want to hear about the tides, plankton, or whales? It's so vast that it's almost an impossible question. However, in its simplest form, great marketing bridges the gap between your business and your customers, allowing them to understand how you can help them.

## IT'S ALL ABOUT THE CUSTOMER

The customer is selfish. We all are. When we are asked to part with our precious time or money, we want to know, "What's in it for me?"

The clearer you are in your messaging, the easier it will be for your offer to resonate with the right people and get them to understand immediately how much your product or service can help them. I go a little nuts when I hear business owners say they just need to get the word out about their company. No. No, you don't. You want to get the *right* words out—words that emotionally resonate with your target market because that leads to sales.

If you want a great resource to help with your messaging, I consider *Building a StoryBrand* by Donald Miller to be the Holy Grail of marketing books. Fortunately for me, I applied the excellent strategies they teach when I was growing my legal software company. This book will walk you step by step through concepts such as positioning your customer as the hero and the importance of clear messaging. Since I had already seen how powerful these concepts were in growing a business, when I found this book with them so beautifully explained, I was positively marketing-geek-giddy!

As a general rule, our brains are lazy (or, more kindly put, trying to conserve resources), so don't expect a potential customer to make giant leaps to figure out who you are, what you offer, and how they will be better off with your product. Straightforward, simple, and clear will win every time. If you are not sure whether your messaging is clear enough, here's a test you can run. Find an eight-year-old and show them your website. If they can't tell you what you do in under a minute, it's too complicated, and you need to simplify your messaging.

Some great questions to ask yourself that can help you craft a meaningful message are:

- Why would someone need my product or service?

- How will my product help them survive and thrive?
- What will their life be like with my product or service?
- What will life be like without my product or service?

## SO . . . WHAT DO YOU DO?

A power move to spend time on is creating a captivating and powerful response to the question, "So, what do you do?" Whether you are asked this in an elevator or on a national podcast, you want to be able to clearly convey what you do, who you do it for, why you do it, and the amazing outcome you create for people.

We've all been on the receiving end (and maybe guilty of) the dreaded rambling mess response. You know what I am talking about—the person you meet at a networking mixer who responds to this question with, "Well, I do this. I do that. But then I do this and sometimes this other thing. Oh, I forgot to mention . . ."

At best, a sloppy response makes us forgettable. At worst, we lose business because we come across as scattered and untrustworthy. An additional bummer is the listener doesn't have a clear notion of what we do and who we do it for, so they can't refer us. Even if this person is not a potential customer, they could bump into a perfect client for us in their next meeting. You don't want to miss out on these opportunities just because you haven't spent the time to work out a great response. I highly recommend *Marketing Made Simple,* also by Donald Miller, to help you craft a message that will be a powerful sales tool for you.

## PROGRESS, NOT PERFECTION

It's easy to get hung up on our marketing and use this as an excuse to delay the sometimes terrifying step that is launching our business (or perhaps a new product or service). When I was eighteen and a freelance trumpet player, my business card was amazing. At least, I thought it was. It had great colors, fancy graphics, and a whole bunch of words demonstrating everything I could do. It took the better part of a day with a graphic designer to get it just right.

Shortly afterward, I met one of the most famous trumpet players in the world, and he handed me his business card. It was simply his name, the word "trumpet," and his phone number in black and white. I felt like an idiot but learned a valuable lesson that things don't need to be fancy to work.

Of course, we want our marketing to look great and represent us well. But getting obsessive over it is an easy trap to fall into and will keep you from making that all-important forward progress. I like to tell people that no matter how much you agonize over what you put out there, you'll likely want to redo it in a year anyway, so just do your best with what you've got now.

## WHAT'S A SALES FUNNEL?

Your sales funnel is a model of the journey people go through to become your customer. And just like any journey, we want it to be a pleasant one where our potential customer feels comfortable and confident that they know where they are going with the occasional delight of being handed a warm towel or complimentary drink. We don't want them to feel abandoned or frustrated trying to figure out how to navigate on their own and guessing where they need to go next. Having a mess of a sales process is inefficient and irritating, not only for you but also for your potential client.

In its most basic form, a sales funnel consists of three stages: leads, prospects, and customers. Though the stages can be called other things, and your funnel may have more stages than this, the concept is the same. People enter your funnel as leads at the top, continue to be nurtured as prospects, and come out of the bottom as a customer. Of course, some people may exit your sales funnel (at any stage), which is still a healthy part of the process.

## The Top of the Funnel

The top of the funnel is generally considered the lead or awareness stage. In this stage, the potential customer knows who you are but needs to learn more. They might have seen an ad or signed up for your lead magnet, such as a free download or video. That is a low-risk opt-in to get to know your business better.

## The Middle of the Funnel

The next stage is the prospect or interest phase. Here is where your potential customer is taking you more seriously and actively exploring whether you are the right business to help them. It may mean taking you up on a free consultation or attending a webinar. All these things are a further step to find out if you can solve their problem.

## The Bottom of the Funnel

The bottom of your funnel is where the commitment happens and money changes hands. However, this is not where the process ends. Making sure a customer is delighted and becomes a raving fan is a fantastic way to not only set up a long-lasting relationship with this client but will hopefully inspire them to refer you to their friends as well.

No matter how you ultimately set up your funnel, make sure you are building your email list.

The ultimate goal for your sales funnel system is uninterrupted flow. No matter how many stages of this funnel you need, potential customers need to flow smoothly through (or exit) with as little friction as possible.

What is friction? It's anything that interrupts your customers otherwise enjoyable journey down your sales funnel. Pretty much anything that annoys, delays, or inconveniences the client is friction. Find and anticipate all those points of friction and remove them from your sales funnel process.

Another great thing about having a sales funnel is that it allows you to predict future revenue. For example, if you find that it takes a hundred leads to convert to fifty prospects, who then convert to twenty-five sales, you can then predict how many sales you will have based on how many leads are currently in your funnel. Many Customer Relationship Management (CRM) software programs have this process built in for you.

By knowing this information, you can increase sales by getting more leads and improving your conversion rates at each stage of the funnel. The more people who convert from each stage to the next, the more money you make!

## COMMUNICATE WITH CARE

I'm naturally hyper and tend to speak quickly. However, if I'm meeting with a person who is more reserved and speaks slower, I intentionally slow my pace to match theirs. If I were to barrel ahead at my normal pace, I'd end up annoying the crud out of them and potentially losing the sale and harming the relationship. To communicate effectively, we need to care enough to adapt to our clients.

I have to admit, I found this torturous at first, and on many a sales call, I wanted to scream, "Please, for the love of God, speed up!" But by matching my communication style to better fit theirs, I was able to promote clear and honest communication, which led to many rewarding long-term relationships (and sales). Dedicate time to learn how to communicate effectively and be a great listener. There are very few things out there that will give you a greater return on your investment.

# 7

## Get Ready to Grow

*"Start from wherever you are and with whatever you've got."*

Jim Rohn

If you are like many small business owners starting out, saying your marketing budget is tight would likely be generous. So how the heck do you start gaining traction and getting clients without the funds to do it?

I'm here to tell you not only is it possible, but I've self-funded and grown businesses for many years on a shoestring budget. Though a limited budget can seem like a huge obstacle, there are some benefits. One plus is that you are always super careful to make sure that your money is working as hard for you as it possibly can. That forces you to make careful (and sometimes painful) decisions for the betterment of your business.

When you have financial resources, it's easier to prolong problems than make the difficult decisions needed to solve them. Using money as a crutch to sustain your business rather than addressing the underlying issues can actually cause a business to fail. For example, letting employees go is always difficult (especially when they're family!). When an employee is a great person but not a good fit for your company, you carry them to the detriment of your business. So, though a lack of money is certainly a challenge, the grass isn't always greener.

If your funds are limited, you have to get creative. Some businesses do need funding to start, but if you don't have huge and immediate needs for staff, space, and equipment, there are awesome ways to grow on a limited to non-existent budget.

What tactics work best for your business growth will depend on you and your strengths and preferences, as well as your market. If you are a gifted writer or speaker, use those talents to your advantage. If you don't enjoy a particular marketing activity, you'll naturally avoid it, so find an option that truly works for you.

I once coached a teacher who dreaded recording videos without any audience feedback. Her solo videos weren't bad; they simply lacked the exuberance she had during her weekly teaching sessions. I asked what prevented her from putting out recorded video segments from when she did have a live audience, and the answer was "nothing." Problem solved! She no longer had to avoid and dread recording those solo videos, *and* it saved her time because she was repurposing what she was already doing. So, get creative, use your strengths, and find ways to market that you enjoy!

## BANK ON THE BASICS

Before you start driving traffic with paid marketing, cover your basics first. Here are some foundational ways to connect with customers looking for what you offer:

### Investing in SEO (Search Engine Optimization) Help

Though I am no technical or online advertising guru by any stretch of the imagination, I thought it always made sense to make sure people who are already looking for my type of business could find me—before investing in paid ads. That's why I suggest people invest in making sure to optimize their website for search engines. If you've had someone help you with your website, they might already have this covered for you. If not, get some quotes from a few experts so they can set you up for success.

### Optimize Search Engines

Another area where you will want to invest some time and effort is setting up your business correctly with search engines like Google. You can get fancy here, but for starters, make sure your customers can find you, get a great impression of your company, and can contact you directly in a few clicks. Investing a bit of time to get this set up right will be well worth it. Since this is not my area of expertise, these are the types of experts I routinely bring on in my free Facebook Group, The Women's Small Business & Leadership Network, and you are welcome to join us.

### Customer Referrals and Word of Mouth

If you provide massive value to your customers and create raving fans, you are building the most powerful sales force you could hope for. Do all you can to encourage your customers to refer you and make it easy for them to do so. Don't just wish and hope you get referred, but actively build into your sales process a system for encouraging referrals.

### Email Marketing

No matter how much social media reach you have, make sure you build your email list. Your email list is a business asset you control, so you won't have to start from scratch if any particular platform goes away or something happens to your account. Since your social media efforts are not guaranteed to be seen by your audience, email is a great way to cut through the noise.

There is low-cost and even free email marketing software available to help you build your list the right way and stay in compliance with the CAN-SPAM ACT of 2003 (yes, this is an actual legal thing!). These products also offer a host of automation features, such as the ability to build personalized campaigns and nurture sequences, which will help your email marketing be more effective.

One of the powers of email is the ability to keep nurturing the relationships you have with both your potential clients and customers by providing value. Email is the perfect place to share your videos, blog posts, and insider offers. And by showing up consistently in their inbox, you remain top-of-mind. So even if your potential customer was not ready to buy when they signed up for your list, if your email comes in when they do need your product or service, you will be the one to call!

## FANTASTICALLY FREE

My dad used to say, "there's no such thing as a free lunch," but using social media to grow your business is likely the closest thing to a free lunch we're ever going to get. Though social media is certainly a great tool to use, there are other free options to take advantage of as well.

### Creating a Facebook Group

Creating a Facebook Group is an exceptional way to grow your business if you are a natural connector. You are not only positioning yourself as an expert but also creating an audience and community of potential customers. It's also an exceptional way to get feedback during your creation process to develop products your audience wants and needs. Launching a product into a group of your fans, knowing you'll get sales, is a truly beautiful thing. Building my community, The Women's Small Business & Leadership Network, has been a lot of work but incredibly rewarding!

### Leverage Social Media

Social media is an incredible way to reach customers but can be overwhelming. My advice here is to determine which platform your customers use and make a go of it there first. Wonderfully, some platforms allow you to cross-promote with ease, but certainly do not try to master *all* of the social media platforms at once. It's just too much.

Once you've mastered one, then, by all means, conquer another. Just like we don't learn five languages at once, concentrate your efforts on your best guess that will provide you the most return on your investment of time.

## Networking Both Online and in Person

A carefully cultivated network is an incredible business asset, because doing business is always about people. Sales expert Bob Burg says, "All things being equal; people will do business with and refer business to, those people they know, like, and trust." We all know this is true when we drive ten miles out of our way to go to our trusted mechanic and pass by five others which are technically more convenient.

Networking is not just for finding individual clients. You can network to find referral sources. For example, if you are a health coach, you could seek out medical practices in need of a great person to refer their patients.

When networking online, my biggest tip is regardless of the platform you're using, make sure that your profile is optimized and has clear links to your business. I see people on Facebook all the time who are contributing to groups like crazy in hopes of gaining business. But when you click on their name to learn more about them, you see nice pictures of their family vacations, but no clear place where you can learn more about their business.

Some platforms have specific rules around selling, so make sure you know what they are. However, do take care to make sure anyone looking at you knows how to easily take the next step to connect with your business.

## Community Bulletin Boards, Online and Physical

When I gave birth to my son, I needed help with house cleaning, especially since he came by C-section, being the nine-pound-fifteen-ounce amazing meatball-head that he was. So, I tore off one of those little strips of paper from an ad posted on a bulletin board outside my supermarket.

This lovely woman was my cleaner for six years, and she ended up working for my mother, my brother, and at least two of my friends for more than five years each. That's a pretty good return on investment for an 8 ½" x 11" sheet of paper thumbtacked to a wall.

Of course, there are also online equivalents to this, including local community pages. See what their rules are on promotion and get your name out there.

## Free Publicity

Journalists need content like the rest of us, so if you have an interesting story, reach out to the news outlets in your area to let them know. If you are interested in media coverage, what could you do in your business that might be noteworthy and newsworthy? For example, could you donate your services, host a community event, or create a scholarship?

You can also create a press release and upload it to a trusted distribution service, or you could use a service like HARO (which stands for "Help a Reporter Out") to get some press.

## LOW-COST LEVERAGE

Though anyone trying to sell you advertising will disagree, marketing does not have to cost you an arm and a leg. There are many low-cost marketing techniques you can take advantage of to grow your business, such as:

### Blogging

Another wonderful way to deliver massive value is by creating great content that helps your target audience. Whether you are a landscaper warning homeowners about poisonous plants, or a health coach helping your clients drink enough water, we all love and appreciate great advice.

I truly appreciate the email that my veterinarian sends monthly with links to their blog, and their advice even saved my cat. Before subscribing to their blog, I had no idea that some essential oils were toxic to kitties, and I had just received some as a gift! Because of their excellent content, I'm constantly forwarding their articles to my friends and family, some of whom have become customers because of it.

I also have my favorite food bloggers I return to time and time again for recipes for my culinary-challenged life. When they have a new cookbook out, I always take notice, buy one for myself and gift additional copies because I appreciate their helpful content. Our goal is to create this kind of loyalty for our business too.

Direct Mail

Did you know you can buy a mailing list of your target customers? It's a bit old school, but it still works, especially for people struggling to grow their businesses solely online. For example, if you are a local yoga studio and you've determined you are trying to reach married women between the ages of 35 and 47 with an interest in health and wellness and who live within a 12-mile radius from your studio, you can buy a list for that. You can get as fancy and expensive as mailing a bulky gift or as simple and inexpensive as a postcard or letter you write and send from home.

Studies have found that direct mail creates a 20 percent greater motivation to purchase than digital media, and the return on investment on average is around 15 percent.[1] If your current marketing efforts aren't getting you to your goals, try adding direct mail as a tool to build your brand. If you do buy a list, make sure you review their terms of use. Most times, you can reuse that list and mail to it many times for that one-time investment.

Joint Marketing Collaborations

Joint marketing can be so much fun! There are many ways to collaborate for the benefit of both businesses. If you know of someone who has a complementary product or service for your target market, see what fun ideas you can come up with to collaborate. Whether it's free samples, discounts, or guest appearances, the options are endless.

Since being connected in my free Facebook Group, a breathing expert paired up with a sacred dance teacher for a fantastic, informative, and fun seminar. It's a win-win-win scenario as both experts benefit from sharing their audiences, and the clients win with a great seminar to attend. These collaborations also give you a built-in accountability partner while lowering your costs by sharing expenses. I just *love* these opportunities!

[1] https://www.canadapost.ca/assets/pdf/blogs/CPC_Neuroscience_EN_150717.pdf.

### Craft, Local Fairs, and Trade Shows

These events are a great way to build awareness about your business, get first-hand feedback on your products, and find out what questions people have about your services. Use this feedback to improve your products and make sure your marketing addresses the questions being asked.

Also, if you can, carefully choose where your display will be. Ideally, this will be in an area where there's plenty of foot traffic. I've attended many of these, and it's disheartening when you are sitting far away from the action.

## MAKE MONEY MARKETING

Yes, you can get paid to market your business. It's a fabulous way to go. Some options to explore are:

### Speaking

Speaking is a fantastic way to build your brand, reach a larger audience, and position yourself as a trusted expert. If you choose to invest your time to improve your speaking skills, you'll even be able to command a speaking fee. So yes, you will be getting paid to market your business!

If you need help with your public speaking skills, Toastmasters International is an incredibly supportive public speaking training program. If you are looking to speak on podcasts, check out the Facebook Group, "Find a Guest, Be a Guest."

## Community Grants

There's a wonderful program in my home state called the Massachusetts Cultural Council that provides grants to anyone looking to provide value to the community. If you have a service you can share or teach, you can submit a grant application in any community where you'd like to feature your expertise. Your event (and therefore your company) can also be promoted in the local media sources—usually for *free*! Take a look within your state's own community services to see if it offers any similar programs.

## Hosting Webinars, Classes, and Networking Events

I'll let you in on a secret. I created a networking group by accident. I love connecting people and bringing resources together to help women in business. When I started the Women's Small Business & Leadership Network, I was thinking about us all connecting, supporting, and growing our businesses solely online.

That was until my wonderful friend Tammy asked me, "When is your next event?" Well, a few months later, thirty of us were sipping wine together at another member's urban winery, making valuable business connections and friendships. Happy accidents are the best! So are opportunities for you to bring others together.

## FREE SAMPLES, TRIALS, AND MONEY-BACK GUARANTEES

When we make a purchase decision, there is a level of risk involved. If we can lower this risk for our potential customers, the decision to purchase is easier, and it also aids in preventing buyer's remorse.

This lesson was driven home to me when I was eight years old. For years, my nana had raved about this amazing ice cream flavor she had when she was a kid called tutti frutti. Though I thought it was long extinct, one day, we ended up at an out-of-the-way shop that carried it.

Many of you will appreciate the high-pressure ice cream decision that was before me. Should I risk trying something new that I might hate or stay safe with what I know I love? Well, I went for it. I ordered a big bowl of tutti frutti . . . and it was the most wretched substance I had ever tasted. Not only did it taste totally gross, but it also had additional bonus bits of fruitcake-like-chunks that were floating around in my mouth. I don't know what on earth people were thinking in the 1930s when this stuff was apparently popular, but it was disgusting! Talk about buyer's remorse.

Just think: I would not be writing about how horrid this product was 35 years later if the ice cream shop had only offered a tiny spoon sample. Letting your potential client taste a little bit of what you have going on or offering a money-back guarantee helps ensure your customer is getting just what they want (and not tutti frutti!)

## MEASURE YOUR MARKETING

Missing the mark at some point is unavoidable, and it can be incredibly stressful when you need to get money in the door. To help you make good decisions, you need to track your marketing as best you can. There are many technical ways to help you with this, but I'll even accept you putting hash marks in a notebook.

The old adage is true—you can't manage what you don't measure. So, make sure you measure your marketing returns over time to see what is working and what isn't. It's a hard line to walk because you don't want to give up too early in some marketing endeavors. In this noisy marketplace, a consumer needs to see you a lot before they reach out. However, if you track your progress, you can adjust and get better results faster.

# 8

# Taking Care of Your Most Precious Business Asset You!

*"If you feel 'burnout' setting in, if you feel demoralized and exhausted, it is best, for the sake of everyone, to withdraw and restore yourself."*

Dalai Lama

As an entrepreneur, solopreneur, or any kind of "*-preneur*," you need to take care of yourself to take care of business. The demands of launching and growing a company are huge. They require the best of you emotionally, physically, and mentally.

## A HEALTHY BUSINESS STARTS WITH A HEALTHY OWNER

One of my mantras is a healthy business starts with a healthy owner. Driven women like us are *way* too good about forging ahead no matter the cost and just plain putting ourselves last in the process. It's tricky because we need a heck of a lot of grit to achieve our success. But when we take our efforts to the extreme, it backfires big time as we run ourselves into the ground.

I'm an advocate of changing how we look at entrepreneurship. We envision and embrace the long hours, skipping meals, and drinking gallons of coffee like a badge of honor and rite of passage. But you can't eat a bag of Doritos for lunch, have a Diet Coke for dinner, get home late, drink a few glasses of wine, stay up working until three o'clock in the morning, and last for the long haul. You're going to feel awful; your performance will suffer, and it will negatively impact your business.

I know many women who take care of their cars better than their bodies! They wouldn't expect their car to perform well, filling the gas tank with junk and never servicing it, but they expect it from themselves. Let's pledge to hold each other accountable and give ourselves permission to take excellent care of ourselves.

## THE ENTREPRENEURIAL ATHLETE

I was recently talking to a wonderful entrepreneur friend in the midst of a huge startup. The conversation went to how many hours would be required at this stage. We discussed ways to lessen the load, but there was truly so much to get done. Our talk then turned to how unhealthily she was eating and how little sleep she was getting.

I reminded her, especially at this stage, she had to treat herself like an elite athlete. I'm honored to know many athletes and how hard they train. Taking superb care of their body is a top priority because they know their success depends on it. We have the same need to fuel our bodies and minds for optimal performance, but it's a perspective we owners lack. Taking care of ourselves is something we do "when we have time." And as we know, if we don't make the time, it never comes.

Even though it is tempting to skip a meal or eat unhealthy food when you feel rushed, it is counterproductive to your goals. Your body won't have what it needs to work right. I'm talking from experience here. Your body needs care, and your brain is particularly expensive to run, so make sure you feed it accordingly. We have no choice but to respect that.

I know we all feel invincible (at least to a certain age). We feel like we can run on fumes for days, weeks, or years hustling after the dream. I felt that way until I ran myself into the ground building my legal software company.

## LISTEN WHEN YOUR BODY TALKS

Being a workaholic and a new mom is not a good combination. I was recovering from a C-section, struggling to care for my newborn baby, and in retrospect, I should have arranged for more help and care. But I was suffering from the delusion, like many women, that I should be able to do it all. That all happened while navigating my legal software company through the Great Recession of 2007–2009. I was under a lot of stress.

When it comes to your body and health, my wonderful naturopathic doctor tells it to me this way. Your body will start to whisper to you, then it will shout, and if you haven't listened yet, it will drop you to your knees. Oh boy, was I dropped.

Figuring out what was wrong with me wasn't helped by the fact that my symptoms were all over the place. Every noise was excruciatingly loud. I couldn't move my neck. My arms would go numb. My speech was slurred, and I'd wake up every morning at three a.m. and dry heave for hours. My heart would randomly skip beats, and everything at night was blurry. I was also plagued by debilitating joint pain, fatigue, and exhaustion.

To make matters worse, no doctor could tell me what was wrong. They brushed me off, saying that it was because I was stressed as a new mom and not so subtly suggested that it was all in my head, even as my symptoms got worse. I *was* stressed, but I knew something much more was going on.

After months of searching, I found an article that linked hypersensitivity to noise as a symptom of a severe magnesium deficiency. The more I read, the more things fell into place: the slurred speech, the tingling and numbness, the heart arrhythmia. Not to mention, this nutrient deficiency can be exacerbated by prolonged periods of stress. I finally had an answer.

From then on, it was all uphill, but I never again took my health or nutritional needs for granted. Within a few years, I was able to rebuild myself back to a healthier version of myself than had ever existed before. I even got a certification as a holistic nutritionist to be a confident advocate for women small business owners getting adequate nutrition.

I joke that the only speech I could give on this topic would be "What I learned about work-life balance by doing everything wrong!" I realized I couldn't out-think or out-will my body's needs. And neither can you. If you're not consuming the nutrition you need, your body won't work at the cellular level. It doesn't matter how driven, stubborn, or smart you are; you can't out-think nutritional deficiencies. You must consume the proper nutrients because they are the foundational building blocks for your cells to function. Now, I do my best to treat and feed myself like the elite entrepreneurial athlete I am!

## YOUR INVISIBLE ARMY

Feeling utterly alone is a miserable feeling known to many of us, especially solopreneurs. I want to share an exercise that has helped me and many others remind ourselves that although we may feel alone, that is rarely the case.

You'll need a piece of poster board and a container of those little paper hearts they sell at craft stores (or Post-it notes will do too). Put your name on one and stick it right in the middle of your board. Next, one by one, write down the names of all the people who love and support you on the hearts, including pets, family, friends, the nice lady at the coffee shop who smiles at you every morning and stick them on the board around your name.

I don't care who you write down, even if it's "coffee shop lady" or "guy that waves to me on my way to work." If they are connected to you in a positive way, stick them on the board. You can get fancy if you want to put more significant connections closer to your name in the center if you like—really, just do whatever your heart desires. You can't do this wrong. And you can even stick me on your board because I believe in you, and if you are reading the words on this page, we are connected, and I'm sending you love.

Once you've written your hearts and stuck them to your poster board, prop it up somewhere and stand back. What do you see? Hopefully, you see a lot of love and support you have that you didn't realize was there. When you are feeling alone, it's easy to believe that you *are* alone. You may feel there's nobody around you and nobody to support you. Many of us have a small army and don't even realize it. So, make this visual representation of the army supporting you and stick it somewhere you can see it every morning.

## FREEING YOURSELF FROM GUILT

Do you feel guilty 24-7? When you are with your kids, do you feel guilty you aren't working? When you're working, do you feel guilty you aren't with your kids? And when you take time for yourself, do you feel guilty you aren't being productive or doing something else?

I once asked my wonderful friend and mindfulness teacher Lisa Campbell how to break this awful cycle of 24-7 guilt. Her answer was mindfulness. She advocates blocking everything out and being fully present in whatever you're doing. If you're with your kids, be fully present with your kids. If you're at work, be fully present at work. It's no fun to constantly feel like you are being torn in two. Starting the shift to being fully present allows you to let that guilt go and enjoy your life so much more.

# 9

# Investing in Yourself

*"Investing in yourself
is the best investment
you will ever make.
It will not only improve your life,
it will improve the lives of all those
around you."*

Robin Sharma

If there were a shortcut to success, would you take it? Well, that, my friends, is what happens when you have the right coaches and mentors in your life. Sometimes, we can talk ourselves out of coaching due to the expense or the false belief we can figure it all out on our own, but we fail to calculate the cost of *not* having a coach or mentor.

When I was in the startup phase of my legal software company, I was broke. I mean, sitting on an upside-down bucket, eating ramen, can't afford a Christmas tree kind of broke. However, I knew I was over my head and desperately needed experienced help. The coach I found who I believed could help me was $500 per month. To my barely-surviving self, this was an astronomical amount of money at the time.

The cost of hiring him was scary, but the cost of *not* hiring him and losing my business was scarier. Somehow, I scrounged up the money, which was the best decision I ever made because it saved our company. Now, whatever area of life I want to see significant progress in, I hire a coach. It's one of the very few shortcuts to success that exists.

## YOU ARE WORTH IT

Another challenge we women can have in our quest for success is spending money on ourselves. Especially *a lot* of money. The kids, the employees, the house repairs will always seem more urgent. You need to build self-development into your budget so you don't get the leftovers of life. Whenever I have invested in myself to get to the next level I wanted to achieve, it's always been a scary amount of money, but it has never let me down.

Now, I have several coaches. Some are short term. Some are long term. I use coaches strategically to help get the best out of me, speed up the learning curve, and avoid costly mistakes. I might be working with three or four coaches who all specialize in very specific things, but all of that is to keep me moving forward as efficiently as possible.

## HOW TO FIND THE RIGHT COACH

First, determine if you are looking for a coach, teacher, mentor, consultant, or a little bit of everything. What are the differences? A teacher is an expert in an area who will instruct you on what they know so you can do it too. A mentor has the personal experience they can share and offer guidance. A coach is someone who helps you internally explore the answers to your challenges and find solutions, work through your fears, set goals, and help hold you accountable for achieving them and modifying them when needed. A consultant is someone with a deep understanding of your particular challenge. You are usually paying them to take a look at your situation so you can get their recommendation.

When you hire a coach, do your due diligence, ask questions, and get references. Sign up for a free consulting call and interview them to see if they are a good fit for you and can meet your needs professionally and personally. Even if they have great credentials on paper, you might enjoy someone with a more rigid, no-B.S. personality, while someone else might find that style too abrasive. You might want someone who feels more nurturing. Choose someone who feels right to you.

Since coaching is not a highly-regulated industry, you have to be careful. Just because a business coach gives themselves a fancy title and has slick marketing doesn't mean they're experienced or know what they're doing. I cannot tell you how many business coaches I've seen confidently advertising and telling us how to run our business but who have little to no successful business experience of their own. It personally drives me *nuts* and is one of my greatest motivators to write this book.

## KEEP MOVING FORWARD

It's hard to get something right the first time. Just like a child learning how to walk, you will stumble a bit when you are just starting out. I don't think I know a successful entrepreneur who hasn't, myself included. It's all part of being on the entrepreneurial journey. But if you keep picking yourself up and moving forward, you'll gain confidence, meet some great friends along the way, and start to run together.

Starting a small business, and quite honestly every stage of entrepreneurship, requires calculated risk and constant steps outside of your comfort zone. Feelings of fear, doubt, and considering quitting are all normal. But there is far greater risk in not following your dreams and living a life you don't love.

If you hold firm to your vision, you'll be living a life true to yourself and enjoying the incredible fulfillment that comes with it. So, keep moving forward toward your dreams. You've got this!

# Final Thoughts and Resources

*"Some leaders are born women."*

Geraldine Ferraro

Though it can be a crazy ride that will test everything you've got, you truly have what it takes to be a successful entrepreneur. I have faith in you that if you step onto the path of entrepreneurial adventure, and keep moving along that path, whatever you need to succeed will find its way to you. Wherever you are, start with whatever you have, and create your dream!

And totally write to me at dani@daniwhitestone.com to let me know how it's going!

With much love and gratitude,

☺ Dani

## BOOKS TO INSPIRE AND EDUCATE

*The Confidence Gap: A Guide to Overcoming Fear and Self-Doubt,* Russ Harris

*StoryBrand* and *Marketing Made Simple*, Donald Miller

*How to Win Friends and Influence People*, Dale Carnegie

*You Are a Badass at Making Money*, Jen Sincero

*Think and Grow Rich*, Napoleon Hill

*The Magnesium Miracle*, Carolyn Dean

*The 1-Page Marketing Plan,* Allan Dib

## WEBSITES AND RESOURCES

Meditation exercises from Lisa Campbell, https://mindfulfilled.com/guided-meditations/

Public Speaking Training—Toastmasters International, https://www.toastmasters.org/

## CONNECT WITH ME

You are welcome to join me and my amazing entrepreneur friends in the Women's Small Business & Leadership Network Community. Find us at www.daniwhitestone.com/connect

You can also connect with me at
www.daniwhitestone.com

and write to me at
dani@daniwhitestone.com.

# ACKNOWLEDGMENTS

I'd like to thank my son, Tristan, for his constant love and support and for emptying the dishwasher. My business partner, Tom, for always supporting me when I'm taking a leap of faith and talking me down when I'm freaking out on most of them. My English Mastiff, Atlas, for ten years of unconditional love, support, drool, and hugs. My parents, Ellen and Michael Mulryan, for raising me to be an independent, strong woman who does crazy things to pursue her dreams. And thank you to my nieces and nephews, Parker, Corwin, Arwen, Willow, Evan, Mila, Annie, and Cecilia, so that you could see your name in a book. ☺

Thank you to Dennis McCurdy, Honorée Corder, Alice Sullivan, Dino Marino and Terry Stafford who helped make this book a reality!

To all the women of the Women's Small Business & Leadership Facebook Group and my amazing Business Builder Community, you are my inspiration! Thank you for all your wisdom, vibrancy, humor, and support. I am so incredibly proud to be among you on this entrepreneurial journey.

## ABOUT DANI

Dani Whitestone is a small business coach and founder of the Women's Small Business & Leadership Network. She has a passion for helping women live life on their own terms through building their own small business because she knows how awesome and possible it is.

She is also the sole female cofounder of TurboLaw Software which she helped lead from startup though acquisition.

In addition to decades of entrepreneurial experience, she is a certified John Maxwell Trainer, Speaker and Coach as well as a Certified Strategic Life Coach through Tony Robbins and Cloé Madanes.

Dani's pursuit of knowledge leads her on some crazy adventures, the last of which was competing in an international competition for tai chi sword in Taiwan. Though she does embrace doing crazy things, she's just as content to read by the fire with her amazing son and snoring pug Apollo.

You can find out more at www.daniwhitestone.com.

# AUTHOR'S NOTES

If I could hop in a time machine, this is the book I'd go back and hand to my twenty-year-old struggling entrepreneurial self! I needed a book, *this* book, one that would have given me practical small business advice, some much required guidance, as well as the encouragement I needed to hear as a woman entrepreneur.

Just like many of you, being a driven woman is how we accomplish great things, but also how we run our bodies into the ground if we don't take care of ourselves. I wished I had more self-care woven into all the business books I've read over the years.

Also, for those of you who are teetering on the edge of taking that leap of faith to start your business, I hope this book serves to give you that push you need because you can do this! There's no time like the present to embrace your dream and go for it.

## CONTINUE YOUR JOURNEY

If you'd like to continue your business building journey with me, and reach your goals faster and with less stress, visit www.daniwhitestone.com. I encourage you to check out the **Business Builder Community**. You'll find the support, coaching, education, resources, *and* friendly accountability you need to reach your goals and have your business thrive!

### OUR MEMBERS THRIVE—YOU CAN, TOO!

*"As a female business owner, it is wonderful to have such a fabulous group of women to exchange ideas with and support each other. The Business Builder Coaching Community is essential for any woman who wants to improve herself and her business!"*

–Liz Rawson,
Rawson & Sons Insurance Group, LLC

*"Dani's Business Builder Coaching Community is a wonderful space, especially for the beginner female entrepreneur. Dani shares her business expertise, personal experience, warmth, and honesty on all topics to support your business's growth such as goal setting and marketing strategies. Dani will go out of her way to spotlight, support, and promote your business to help you receive the needed recognition for growth. Dani is all about smart with heart!"*

–Lisa Dahl, Lisa Dahl Wellness

Made in the USA
Columbia, SC
06 June 2021